This Is the Day!

FIVE SONGS FOR THE CHURCH YEAR

BY DORA ANN PURDY

Teaching Highlights by Jeff Reeves

TEACHER'S NOTE
Digital Access to Audio Recordings and PDF files for Singer's Pages and Teaching
Highlights are available for each song in this collection.

EXCLUSIVELY DISTRIBUTED BY

7777 W. BLUEMOUND RD. P.O. BOX 13819 MILWAUKEE, WI 53213

Visit Hal Leonard Online at
www.halleonard.com

Contact Us:
Hal Leonard
7777 West Bluemound Road
Milwaukee, WI 53213
Email: info@halleonard.com

In Europe, contact:
Hal Leonard Europe Limited
1 Red Place
London, W1K 6PL
Email: info@halleonardeurope.com

In Australia contact:
Hal Leonard Australia Pty. Ltd.
4 Lentara Court
Cheltenham, Victoria, 3192 Australia
Email: info@halleonard.com.au

CONTENTS

ALSO AVAILABLE

Sing and Celebrate!
HL35028238

Sing and Celebrate 2!
HL35028755

Sing and Celebrate 3!
HL35029219

Sing and Celebrate 4!
HL35029809

Sing and Celebrate 5!
HL35030476

Sing and Celebrate 6!
HL35031059

Sing and Celebrate 7!
HL35031739

Sing and Celebrate 8!
HL35032293

Sing and Celebrate 9!
HL00295391

Sing and Celebrate 10!
HL00300251

INTRODUCTION

Designed for younger elementary choirs (K-3), *This Is the Day!* contains a variety of songs for general use, Christmas, and Palm Sunday.

Be sure to take advantage of the **digital download resources** (www.halleonard.com/mylibrary). The digital download site features:
- accompaniment and performance tracks
- reproducible singers' pages
- teaching highlights

The teaching highlights help to teach each song and nurture the musical and spiritual development of young singers. Age-appropriate activities make learning fun and memorable.

All digital files are available for digital download. To access the audio MP3's and all PDF files:
- go to: **www.halleonard.com/mylibrary**
- enter the code found on page 1.

This Is the Day! makes a perfect resource for church and parochial school settings.

This Is the Day!

Unison voices and piano

GENERAL WORSHIP

Words based on Psalm 118:24
Additional words by DORA ANN PURDY

Music by
DORA ANN PURDY (ASCAP)

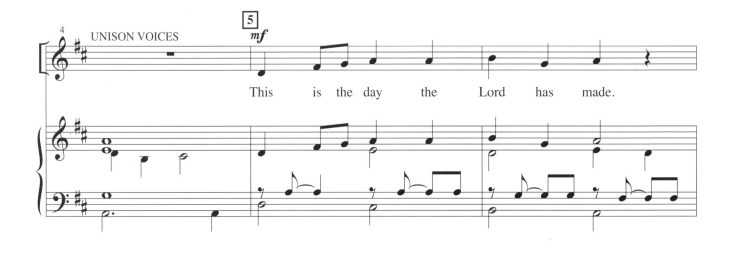

This is the day the Lord has made.

Let us re-joice! Let us re-joice! This is the day the

00527053

* or "God"

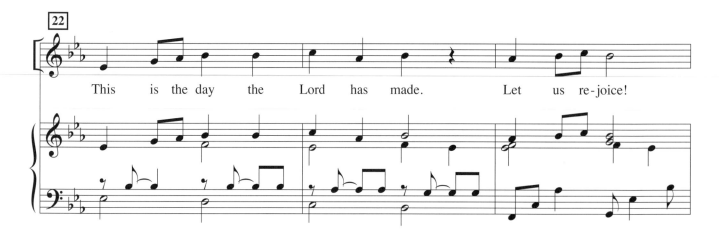

This is the day the Lord has made. Let us re-joice!

Let us re-joice! This is the day the Lord has made.

Let us re-joice and be glad! Let us re-

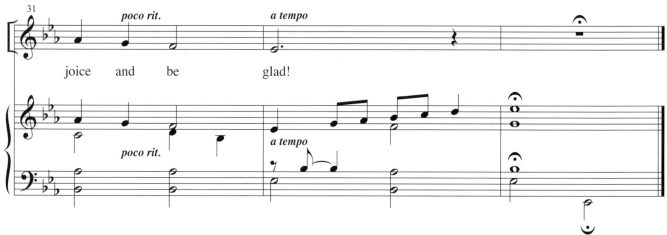

joice and be glad!

Your Word Is a Lamp

Unison voices and piano

GENERAL WORSHIP

Words based on Psalm 118:105
Additional words by DORA ANN PURDY

Music by
DORA ANN PURDY (ASCAP)

00527053

7

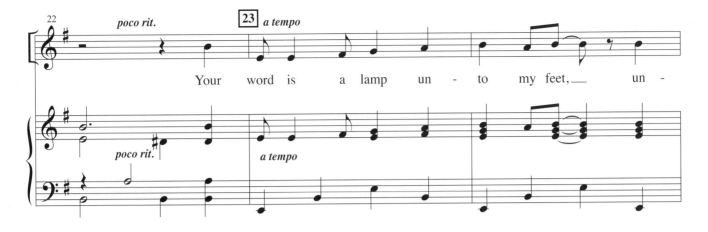

Your word is a lamp un - to my feet,___ un -

to my feet,___ un - to my feet.___ Your word is a lamp un -

to my feet,___ and a light un - to my path, and a

light un - to my path.

00527053

God Is My Refuge and Strength

Unison voices and piano

GENERAL WORSHIP

Words based on Psalm 46:1
Additional words by DORA ANN PURDY

Music by
DORA ANN PURDY (ASCAP)

00527053

00527053

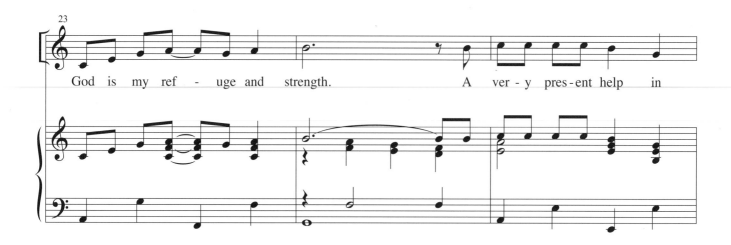

God is my ref - uge and strength. A ver - y pres - ent help in

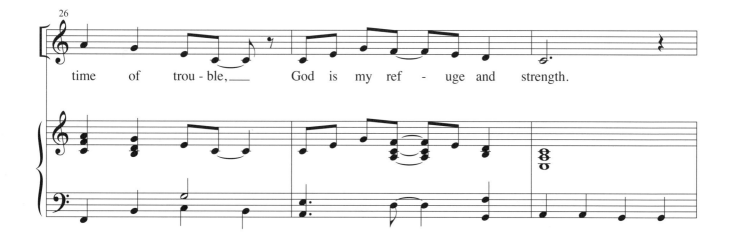

time of trou - ble,__ God is my ref - uge and strength.

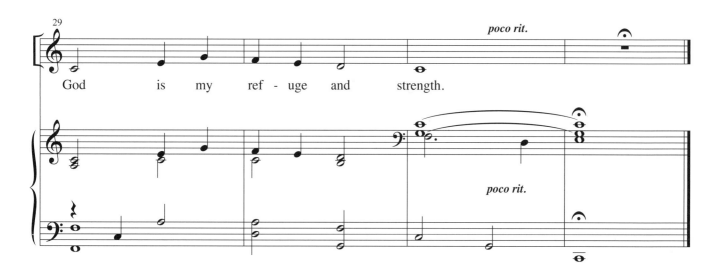

God is my ref - uge and strength.

poco rit.

Gloria!

Unison voices and piano

CHRISTMAS

Words based on the poem,
"Why Do Bells at Christmas Ring?"
by EUGENE FIELD (1850-1895)
Additional words by DORA ANN PURDY

Music by
DORA ANN PURDY (ASCAP)

Performance options:
1. Have the younger children in the group sing only the "Gloria" sections (meas. 5-6, 9-10, 22-23, 26-27, 39-40, 43-44).
2. Use one or more soloists on the verses, if desired.

00527053

Glo-ry to God on high! Once a bright-ly shin-ing star was seen by shep-herds from a-far. It gen-tly moved un-til its light made a man-ger's cra-dle bright. Glo-ri-a! Glo-ri-a!

Lyrics (vocal line):

36 "This is Christ, the ho - ly Child."

39 Glo - ri - a! Glo - ri - a! Glo - ry to God in the

42 high - est! Glo - ri - a! Glo - ri - a! Glo - ry to God on

46 high! Glo - ry to God on high!

* Option: Choir may sing cue size note, instead of lower note, if desired.

00527053

16

Hosanna

Unison voices and piano
with 2 optional handbells or handchimes

PALM SUNDAY

Words and Music by
DORA ANN PURDY (ASCAP)

00527053

Son. Come, sing a song of cheer. Come, sing with

voic - es clear. Wave the palms, clear the way, Christ the King has

HANDBELLS *or*
HANDCHIMES

mf

come   to - day.

00527053

* Option: Choir may sing cue size notes, instead of lower notes, if desired.

00527053

19

GRADE LEVEL SUGGESTIONS AT-A-GLANCE					
SONG TITLE	PAGE	K	1	2	3
Gloria!	13		•	•	•
God Is My Refuge and Strength	10		•	•	•
Hosanna	17	•	•	•	•
This Is the Day!	4		•	•	•
Your Word Is a Lamp	7	•	•	•	•